THE POWERS OF ME THAT BE

3-6-9 CHAKRA AFFIRMATION WORKBOOK

Welcome, Dear Seeker!

You are now embarking upon a practice of profound fulfillment and spiritual awakening. There is no going back from the alchemical transformation you are setting into motion. In this workbook we combine the 3-6-9 Method with Chakra Affirmation Alignment to stimulate The Powers of Me That Be. What, you may ask, are they?

3-6-9 METHOD

This structured approach to writing affirmations three times daily in groups of three, six, and nine is inspired by Nikola Tesla. In his words, "If you only knew the magnificence of the three, six, and nine, then you would have the key to the universe." Regardless of your spiritual outlook, the act of focused repetition will influence your mind. Writing affirmations multiple times reinforces neural pathways, making it easier for the brain to accept and act on your chosen new beliefs.

THE POWERS OF ME THAT BE

In this book we address ourselves to the Powers of Me That Be. These powers could be your own subconscious mind. Your higher self. The god of your traditional faith. The Universe. Source. Gaia, ancestors, angels, guides, elementals, ascended masters, cosmic or interdimensional beings, or any combination of the above. Whatever resonates with you is your Powers of Me That Be. Hold that presence in mind as you write your affirmations.

CHAKRA AFFIRMATION ALIGNMENT

Your body holds seven main chakras, according to Indian spiritual tradition. These centers of energy are linked to different aspects of your being and express specific powers related to your body, mind, and spirit. For a more holistic and cosmic experience, you can phrase your affirmations to tune into the unique vibrations of each chakra. Regardless of your spiritual outlook, finding seven different ways to express a goal produces a robust self-examination and helps to focus and clarify your vision.

WHY WRITE ON PAPER?

Your thoughts and spoken words have power, but when you write you cast a unique kind of spell—you are literally spelling! You strengthen your mind and amplify results by connecting the physical actions of your hands with your mental thoughts and goals, especially when setting spiritual intentions.

Typing on a screen ignites your frontal cortex, or the multitasking part of your brain, and that experience is easily erased or forgotten. Writing on paper engages the deep-focus part of your brain to create a subliminal and lasting impact.

HOW TO USE THIS WORKBOOK

Go to a blank page and use the chakra starter on that page (such as "I am. . .") to craft a clear, concise affirmation. Write your affirmation three times at the start of your day, six times in the middle of your day, and nine times at the end of your day, filling in a total of two pages, left to right, per day. Do this every day until the book is filled.

State your affirmation in the present tense as if it's already happening (*I am attracting abundance into my life*). There are basic sample affirmations throughout the book. Use any one of those or create your own. Write anything that suits your purpose. You can get very specific (*I am North America's tallest and highest-paid ornithological expert*), but if you go a bit more general (*I am celebrated and rewarded for doing work that I love*), that leaves room for the universe to surprise and delight you. Also, it's very important that you're able to believe what you write. You'll get better results with an affirmation that feels plausibly attainable to you (*I am healthy, strong, and successful*) than you will with something that feels absurd to you (*I am the all-time greatest NBA superstar right now*). The longer you practice this, the easier it will be to create detailed, relevant affirmations.

There are seven chakras; each chakra has nine color-coded entries in this book, allowing for sixty-three days of writing. However you choose to approach this book, you will see results so long as you consistently fill in the pages. You may start at the beginning with the first chakra and move through the pages in order, or you may skip around. You may stick to one affirmation topic (such as health, finance, or relationships) and reword your affirmation within each chakra, or you may try different topics as you go. Given the length of this book, you'll see the most intense and direct results by focusing on no more than three specific topics. If there's no one specific topic that requires your focus, you can use this practice to simply uplift yourself with a different affirmation each day; you'll soon see subtle but wonderful benefits throughout your life. Once this book is filled, you may want to get a new copy and keep going. Or, you can simply continue using this method with any blank notebook or journal.

BE CONSISTENT:
Write daily for best results. If you miss a session or miss a day, don't give up. Just pick up where you left off and keep going.

SENSE IT:
Try to attach your affirmation to one or more of your senses as you write. What will your goal look like, sound like, feel like, and so on? What emotions will you feel when it manifests?

BELIEVE:
Trust the scientific evidence that this process will realign your neural pathways to position you for more positive outcomes. Or, trust the spiritual wisdom that universal forces are actively working to bring your desire to fruition. Whether you lean toward science, faith, or both, your belief in this process is its own self-fulfilling prophecy.

I am

This affirmation roots my intentions firmly in the earth, providing a stable foundation.

Threefold Invocation: I arise and declare what I am to the Powers of Me That Be.

1.

2.

3.

Sixfold Affirmation: I pause and repeat what I am to the Powers of Me That Be.

1.

2.

3.

4.

5.

6.

FIRST   ROOT

I am

This affirmation roots my intentions firmly in the earth, providing a stable foundation.

Ninefold Contemplation: I retire and solidify what I am to the Powers of Me That Be.

1.

2.

3.

4.

5.

6.

7.

8.

9.

The first chakra is the Root or *Muladhara*.

It is located at the base of the spine and represents survival, stability, and security. Possible Root affirmations include: *I am grounded and stable. I am financially secure. I am in perfect health and full of vitality. I am safe and protected. I am worthy of love and belonging. I am confident in my ability to thrive. I am grateful for all that I have.*

ROOT  FIRST

I am

This affirmation roots my intentions firmly in the earth, providing a stable foundation.

Threefold Invocation: I arise and declare what I am to the Powers of Me That Be.

1.

2.

3.

Sixfold Affirmation: I pause and repeat what I am to the Powers of Me That Be.

1.

2.

3.

4.

5.

6.

FIRST   ROOT

I am

This affirmation roots my intentions firmly in the earth, providing a stable foundation.

Ninefold Contemplation: I retire and solidify what I am to the Powers of Me That Be.

1.

2.

3.

4.

5.

6.

7.

8.

9.

The first chakra is the Root or *Muladhara*.

It is located at the base of the spine and represents survival, stability, and security.
Possible Root affirmations include: *I am grounded and stable. I am financially secure. I am in perfect health and full of vitality. I am safe and protected. I am worthy of love and belonging. I am confident in my ability to thrive. I am grateful for all that I have.*

ROOT FIRST

I am

This affirmation roots my intentions firmly in the earth, providing a stable foundation.

Threefold Invocation: I arise and declare what I am to the Powers of Me That Be.

1.

2.

3.

Sixfold Affirmation: I pause and repeat what I am to the Powers of Me That Be.

1.

2.

3.

4.

5.

6.

FIRST   ROOT

I am

This affirmation roots my intentions firmly in the earth, providing a stable foundation.

Ninefold Contemplation: I retire and solidify what I am to the Powers of Me That Be.

1.

2.

3.

4.

5.

6.

7.

8.

9.

The first chakra is the Root or *Muladhara*.

It is located at the base of the spine and represents survival, stability, and security. Possible Root affirmations include: *I am grounded and stable. I am financially secure. I am in perfect health and full of vitality. I am safe and protected. I am worthy of love and belonging. I am confident in my ability to thrive. I am grateful for all that I have.*

ROOT FIRST

I am

This affirmation roots my intentions firmly in the earth, providing a stable foundation.

Threefold Invocation: I arise and declare what I am to the Powers of Me That Be.

1.

2.

3.

Sixfold Affirmation: I pause and repeat what I am to the Powers of Me That Be.

1.

2.

3.

4.

5.

6.

FIRST   ROOT

 # I am

This affirmation roots my intentions firmly in the earth, providing a stable foundation.

Ninefold Contemplation: I retire and solidify what I am to the Powers of Me That Be.

1.

2.

3.

4.

5.

6.

7.

8.

9.

The first chakra is the Root or *Muladhara*.

It is located at the base of the spine and represents survival, stability, and security. Possible Root affirmations include: *I am grounded and stable. I am financially secure. I am in perfect health and full of vitality. I am safe and protected. I am worthy of love and belonging. I am confident in my ability to thrive. I am grateful for all that I have.*

ROOT  FIRST

I am

This affirmation roots my intentions firmly in the earth, providing a stable foundation.

Threefold Invocation: I arise and declare what I am to the Powers of Me That Be.

1.

2.

3.

Sixfold Affirmation: I pause and repeat what I am to the Powers of Me That Be.

1.

2.

3.

4.

5.

6.

FIRST   ROOT

I am

This affirmation roots my intentions firmly in the earth, providing a stable foundation.

Ninefold Contemplation: I retire and solidify what I am to the Powers of Me That Be.

1.

2.

3.

4.

5.

6.

7.

8.

9.

The first chakra is the Root or *Muladhara*.

It is located at the base of the spine and represents survival, stability, and security. Possible Root affirmations include: *I am grounded and stable. I am financially secure. I am in perfect health and full of vitality. I am safe and protected. I am worthy of love and belonging. I am confident in my ability to thrive. I am grateful for all that I have.*

ROOT   FIRST

I am

This affirmation roots my intentions firmly in the earth, providing a stable foundation.

Threefold Invocation: I arise and declare what I am to the Powers of Me That Be.

1.

2.

3.

Sixfold Affirmation: I pause and repeat what I am to the Powers of Me That Be.

1.

2.

3.

4.

5.

6.

I am

This affirmation roots my intentions firmly in the earth, providing a stable foundation.

Ninefold Contemplation: I retire and solidify what I am to the Powers of Me That Be.

1.

2.

3.

4.

5.

6.

7.

8.

9.

The first chakra is the Root or *Muladhara*.

It is located at the base of the spine and represents survival, stability, and security.
Possible Root affirmations include: *I am grounded and stable. I am financially secure.
I am in perfect health and full of vitality. I am safe and protected. I am worthy of love and
belonging. I am confident in my ability to thrive. I am grateful for all that I have.*

I am

This affirmation roots my intentions firmly in the earth, providing a stable foundation.

Threefold Invocation: I arise and declare what I am to the Powers of Me That Be.

1.

2.

3.

Sixfold Affirmation: I pause and repeat what I am to the Powers of Me That Be.

1.

2.

3.

4.

5.

6.

FIRST  ROOT

 # I am

This affirmation roots my intentions firmly in the earth, providing a stable foundation.

Ninefold Contemplation: I retire and solidify what I am to the Powers of Me That Be.

1.

2.

3.

4.

5.

6.

7.

8.

9.

The first chakra is the Root or *Muladhara*.

It is located at the base of the spine and represents survival, stability, and security.
Possible Root affirmations include: *I am grounded and stable. I am financially secure.
I am in perfect health and full of vitality. I am safe and protected. I am worthy of love and
belonging. I am confident in my ability to thrive. I am grateful for all that I have.*

ROOT   FIRST

I am

This affirmation roots my intentions firmly in the earth, providing a stable foundation.

Threefold Invocation: I arise and declare what I am to the Powers of Me That Be.

1.

2.

3.

Sixfold Affirmation: I pause and repeat what I am to the Powers of Me That Be.

1.

2.

3.

4.

5.

6.

FIRST  ROOT

 # I am

This affirmation roots my intentions firmly in the earth, providing a stable foundation.

Ninefold Contemplation: I retire and solidify what I am to the Powers of Me That Be.

1.

2.

3.

4.

5.

6.

7.

8.

9.

The first chakra is the Root or *Muladhara*.

It is located at the base of the spine and represents survival, stability, and security.
Possible Root affirmations include: *I am grounded and stable. I am financially secure.
I am in perfect health and full of vitality. I am safe and protected. I am worthy of love and
belonging. I am confident in my ability to thrive. I am grateful for all that I have.*

ROOT   FIRST

I am

This affirmation roots my intentions firmly in the earth, providing a stable foundation.

Threefold Invocation: I arise and declare what I am to the Powers of Me That Be.

1.

2.

3.

Sixfold Affirmation: I pause and repeat what I am to the Powers of Me That Be.

1.

2.

3.

4.

5.

6.

FIRST   ROOT

I am

This affirmation roots my intentions firmly in the earth, providing a stable foundation.

Ninefold Contemplation: I retire and solidify what I am to the Powers of Me That Be.

1.

2.

3.

4.

5.

6.

7.

8.

9.

The first chakra is the Root or *Muladhara*.

It is located at the base of the spine and represents survival, stability, and security.
Possible Root affirmations include: *I am grounded and stable. I am financially secure. I am in perfect health and full of vitality. I am safe and protected. I am worthy of love and belonging. I am confident in my ability to thrive. I am grateful for all that I have.*

ROOT  FIRST

I feel

This affirmation connects my desires with the fluid energies of emotion and creativity, invigorating my spirit.

Threefold Invocation: I arise and declare what I feel to the Powers of Me That Be.

1.

2.

3.

Sixfold Affirmation: I pause and repeat what I feel to the Powers of Me That Be.

1.

2.

3.

4.

5.

6.

SECOND SACRAL

I feel

This affirmation connects my desires with the fluid energies of emotion and creativity, invigorating my spirit.

Ninefold Contemplation: I retire and solidify what I feel to the Powers of Me That Be.

1.

2.

3.

4.

5.

6.

7.

8.

9.

The second chakra is the Sacral or *Svadhisthana*.
It is located in the lower abdomen about two inches below the navel and represents creativity, sexuality, and pleasure.
Possible Sacral affirmations include: *I feel creative and inspired. I feel passionate and alive. I feel pleasure and joy in my body. I feel connected to my emotions. I feel deserving of financial abundance. I feel balanced and at peace. I feel free to express my desires.*

SACRAL SECOND

I feel

This affirmation connects my desires with the fluid energies of emotion and creativity, invigorating my spirit.

Threefold Invocation: I arise and declare what I feel to the Powers of Me That Be.

1.

2.

3.

Sixfold Affirmation: I pause and repeat what I feel to the Powers of Me That Be.

1.

2.

3.

4.

5.

6.

SECOND · SACRAL

I feel

This affirmation connects my desires with the fluid energies of emotion and creativity, invigorating my spirit.

Ninefold Contemplation: I retire and solidify what I feel to the Powers of Me That Be.

1.

2.

3.

4.

5.

6.

7.

8.

9.

The second chakra is the Sacral or *Svadhisthana*.

It is located in the lower abdomen about two inches below the navel and represents creativity, sexuality, and pleasure. Possible Sacral affirmations include: *I feel creative and inspired. I feel passionate and alive. I feel pleasure and joy in my body. I feel connected to my emotions. I feel deserving of financial abundance. I feel balanced and at peace. I feel free to express my desires.*

I feel

This affirmation connects my desires with the fluid energies of emotion and creativity, invigorating my spirit.

Threefold Invocation: I arise and declare what I feel to the Powers of Me That Be.

1.

2.

3.

Sixfold Affirmation: I pause and repeat what I feel to the Powers of Me That Be.

1.

2.

3.

4.

5.

6.

SECOND SACRAL

I feel

This affirmation connects my desires with the fluid energies of emotion and creativity, invigorating my spirit.

Ninefold Contemplation: I retire and solidify what I feel to the Powers of Me That Be.

1.

2.

3.

4.

5.

6.

7.

8.

9.

The second chakra is the Sacral or *Svadhisthana*.
It is located in the lower abdomen about two inches below the navel and represents creativity, sexuality, and pleasure.
Possible Sacral affirmations include: *I feel creative and inspired. I feel passionate and alive.
I feel pleasure and joy in my body. I feel connected to my emotions. I feel deserving of financial
abundance. I feel balanced and at peace. I feel free to express my desires.*

 SACRAL   SECOND

I feel

This affirmation connects my desires with the fluid energies of emotion and creativity, invigorating my spirit.

Threefold Invocation: I arise and declare what I feel to the Powers of Me That Be.

1.

2.

3.

Sixfold Affirmation: I pause and repeat what I feel to the Powers of Me That Be.

1.

2.

3.

4.

5.

6.

SECOND   SACRAL

I feel

This affirmation connects my desires with the fluid energies of emotion and creativity, invigorating my spirit.

Ninefold Contemplation: I retire and solidify what I feel to the Powers of Me That Be.

1.

2.

3.

4.

5.

6.

7.

8.

9.

The second chakra is the Sacral or *Svadhisthana*.
It is located in the lower abdomen about two inches below the navel and represents creativity, sexuality, and pleasure.
Possible Sacral affirmations include: *I feel creative and inspired. I feel passionate and alive. I feel pleasure and joy in my body. I feel connected to my emotions. I feel deserving of financial abundance. I feel balanced and at peace. I feel free to express my desires.*

SACRAL SECOND

I feel

This affirmation connects my desires with the fluid energies of emotion and creativity, invigorating my spirit.

Threefold Invocation: I arise and declare what I feel to the Powers of Me That Be.

1.

2.

3.

Sixfold Affirmation: I pause and repeat what I feel to the Powers of Me That Be.

1.

2.

3.

4.

5.

6.

SECOND SACRAL

I feel

This affirmation connects my desires with the fluid energies of emotion and creativity, invigorating my spirit.

Ninefold Contemplation: I retire and solidify what I feel to the Powers of Me That Be.

1.

2.

3.

4.

5.

6.

7.

8.

9.

The second chakra is the Sacral or *Svadhisthana*.
It is located in the lower abdomen about two inches below the navel and represents creativity, sexuality, and pleasure. Possible Sacral affirmations include: *I feel creative and inspired. I feel passionate and alive. I feel pleasure and joy in my body. I feel connected to my emotions. I feel deserving of financial abundance. I feel balanced and at peace. I feel free to express my desires.*

SACRAL   SECOND

I feel

This affirmation connects my desires with the fluid energies of emotion and creativity, invigorating my spirit.

Threefold Invocation: I arise and declare what I feel to the Powers of Me That Be.

1.

2.

3.

Sixfold Affirmation: I pause and repeat what I feel to the Powers of Me That Be.

1.

2.

3.

4.

5.

6.

SECOND   SACRAL

I feel

This affirmation connects my desires with the fluid energies of emotion and creativity, invigorating my spirit.

Ninefold Contemplation: I retire and solidify what I feel to the Powers of Me That Be.

1.

2.

3.

4.

5.

6.

7.

8.

9.

The second chakra is the Sacral or *Svadhisthana*.
It is located in the lower abdomen about two inches below the navel and represents creativity, sexuality, and pleasure.
Possible Sacral affirmations include: *I feel creative and inspired. I feel passionate and alive. I feel pleasure and joy in my body. I feel connected to my emotions. I feel deserving of financial abundance. I feel balanced and at peace. I feel free to express my desires.*

SACRAL SECOND

I feel

This affirmation connects my desires with the fluid energies of emotion and creativity, invigorating my spirit.

Threefold Invocation: I arise and declare what I feel to the Powers of Me That Be.

1.

2.

3.

Sixfold Affirmation: I pause and repeat what I feel to the Powers of Me That Be.

1.

2.

3.

4.

5.

6.

SECOND SACRAL

I feel

This affirmation connects my desires with the fluid energies of emotion and creativity, invigorating my spirit.

Ninefold Contemplation: I retire and solidify what I feel to the Powers of Me That Be.

1.

2.

3.

4.

5.

6.

7.

8.

9.

The second chakra is the Sacral or *Svadhisthana*.
It is located in the lower abdomen about two inches below the navel and represents creativity, sexuality, and pleasure. Possible Sacral affirmations include: *I feel creative and inspired. I feel passionate and alive. I feel pleasure and joy in my body. I feel connected to my emotions. I feel deserving of financial abundance. I feel balanced and at peace. I feel free to express my desires.*

SACRAL SECOND

I feel

This affirmation connects my desires with the fluid energies of emotion and creativity, invigorating my spirit.

Threefold Invocation: I arise and declare what I feel to the Powers of Me That Be.

1.

2.

3.

Sixfold Affirmation: I pause and repeat what I feel to the Powers of Me That Be.

1.

2.

3.

4.

5.

6.

I feel

This affirmation connects my desires with the fluid energies of emotion and creativity, invigorating my spirit.

Ninefold Contemplation: I retire and solidify what I feel to the Powers of Me That Be.

1.

2.

3.

4.

5.

6.

7.

8.

9.

The second chakra is the Sacral or *Svadhisthana*.
It is located in the lower abdomen about two inches below the navel and represents creativity, sexuality, and pleasure.
Possible Sacral affirmations include: *I feel creative and inspired. I feel passionate and alive.
I feel pleasure and joy in my body. I feel connected to my emotions. I feel deserving of financial
abundance. I feel balanced and at peace. I feel free to express my desires.*

SACRAL SECOND

I feel

This affirmation connects my desires with the fluid energies of emotion and creativity, invigorating my spirit.

Threefold Invocation: I arise and declare what I feel to the Powers of Me That Be.

1.

2.

3.

Sixfold Affirmation: I pause and repeat what I feel to the Powers of Me That Be.

1.

2.

3.

4.

5.

6.

SECOND   SACRAL

I feel

This affirmation connects my desires with the fluid energies of emotion and creativity, invigorating my spirit.

Ninefold Contemplation: I retire and solidify what I feel to the Powers of Me That Be.

1.

2.

3.

4.

5.

6.

7.

8.

9.

The second chakra is the Sacral or *Svadhisthana*.

It is located in the lower abdomen about two inches below the navel and represents creativity, sexuality, and pleasure. Possible Sacral affirmations include: *I feel creative and inspired. I feel passionate and alive. I feel pleasure and joy in my body. I feel connected to my emotions. I feel deserving of financial abundance. I feel balanced and at peace. I feel free to express my desires.*

SACRAL SECOND

I do

This affirmation empowers my will and determination, aligning my actions with my inner strength.

Threefold Invocation: I arise and declare what I do to the Powers of Me That Be.

1.

2.

3.

Sixfold Affirmation: I pause and repeat what I do to the Powers of Me That Be.

1.

2.

3.

4.

5.

6.

THIRD   SOLAR PLEXUS

I do

This affirmation empowers my will and determination, aligning my actions with my inner strength.

Ninefold Contemplation: I retire and solidify what I do to the Powers of Me That Be.

1.

2.

3.

4.

5.

6.

7.

8.

9.

The third chakra is the Solar Plexus or *Manipura*.
It is located in the upper abdomen in the stomach area and represents personal power, self-esteem, and confidence. Possible Solar Plexus affirmations include: *I do act with confidence and clarity. I do achieve my financial goals. I do take care of my health and well-being. I do pursue my passions with determination. I do stand in my personal power. I do believe in my ability to succeed. I do make decisions that align with my values.*

SOLAR PLEXUS  THIRD

I do

This affirmation empowers my will and determination, aligning my actions with my inner strength.

Threefold Invocation: I arise and declare what I do to the Powers of Me That Be.

1.

2.

3.

Sixfold Affirmation: I pause and repeat what I do to the Powers of Me That Be.

1.

2.

3.

4.

5.

6.

THIRD SOLAR PLEXUS

I do

This affirmation empowers my will and determination, aligning my actions with my inner strength.

Ninefold Contemplation: I retire and solidify what I do to the Powers of Me That Be.

1.

2.

3.

4.

5.

6.

7.

8.

9.

The third chakra is the Solar Plexus or *Manipura*.
It is located in the upper abdomen in the stomach area and represents personal power, self-esteem, and confidence.
Possible Solar Plexus affirmations include: *I do act with confidence and clarity. I do achieve my financial goals. I do take care of my health and well-being. I do pursue my passions with determination. I do stand in my personal power. I do believe in my ability to succeed. I do make decisions that align with my values.*

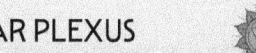

SOLAR PLEXUS   THIRD

I do

This affirmation empowers my will and determination, aligning my actions with my inner strength.

Threefold Invocation: I arise and declare what I do to the Powers of Me That Be.

1.

2.

3.

Sixfold Affirmation: I pause and repeat what I do to the Powers of Me That Be.

1.

2.

3.

4.

5.

6.

THIRD　　　SOLAR PLEXUS

I do

This affirmation empowers my will and determination, aligning my actions with my inner strength.

Ninefold Contemplation: I retire and solidify what I do to the Powers of Me That Be.

1.

2.

3.

4.

5.

6.

7.

8.

9.

The third chakra is the Solar Plexus or *Manipura*.

It is located in the upper abdomen in the stomach area and represents personal power, self-esteem, and confidence. Possible Solar Plexus affirmations include: *I do act with confidence and clarity. I do achieve my financial goals. I do take care of my health and well-being. I do pursue my passions with determination. I do stand in my personal power. I do believe in my ability to succeed. I do make decisions that align with my values.*

SOLAR PLEXUS 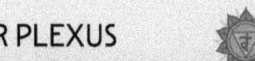 **THIRD**

I do

This affirmation empowers my will and determination, aligning my actions with my inner strength.

Threefold Invocation: I arise and declare what I do to the Powers of Me That Be.

1.

2.

3.

Sixfold Affirmation: I pause and repeat what I do to the Powers of Me That Be.

1.

2.

3.

4.

5.

6.

I do

This affirmation empowers my will and determination, aligning my actions with my inner strength.

Ninefold Contemplation: I retire and solidify what I do to the Powers of Me That Be.

1.

2.

3.

4.

5.

6.

7.

8.

9.

The third chakra is the Solar Plexus or *Manipura*.

It is located in the upper abdomen in the stomach area and represents personal power, self-esteem, and confidence. Possible Solar Plexus affirmations include: *I do act with confidence and clarity. I do achieve my financial goals. I do take care of my health and well-being. I do pursue my passions with determination. I do stand in my personal power. I do believe in my ability to succeed. I do make decisions that align with my values.*

SOLAR PLEXUS THIRD

I do

This affirmation empowers my will and determination, aligning my actions with my inner strength.

Threefold Invocation: I arise and declare what I do to the Powers of Me That Be.

1.

2.

3.

Sixfold Affirmation: I pause and repeat what I do to the Powers of Me That Be.

1.

2.

3.

4.

5.

6.

THIRD   SOLAR PLEXUS

I do

This affirmation empowers my will and determination, aligning my actions with my inner strength.

Ninefold Contemplation: I retire and solidify what I do to the Powers of Me That Be.

1.

2.

3.

4.

5.

6.

7.

8.

9.

The third chakra is the Solar Plexus or *Manipura*.

It is located in the upper abdomen in the stomach area and represents personal power, self-esteem, and confidence. Possible Solar Plexus affirmations include: *I do act with confidence and clarity. I do achieve my financial goals. I do take care of my health and well-being. I do pursue my passions with determination. I do stand in my personal power. I do believe in my ability to succeed. I do make decisions that align with my values.*

SOLAR PLEXUS 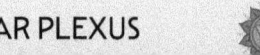 THIRD

I do

This affirmation empowers my will and determination, aligning my actions with my inner strength.

Threefold Invocation: I arise and declare what I do to the Powers of Me That Be.

1.

2.

3.

Sixfold Affirmation: I pause and repeat what I do to the Powers of Me That Be.

1.

2.

3.

4.

5.

6.

THIRD   SOLAR PLEXUS

I do

This affirmation empowers my will and determination, aligning my actions with my inner strength.

Ninefold Contemplation: I retire and solidify what I do to the Powers of Me That Be.

1.

2.

3.

4.

5.

6.

7.

8.

9.

The third chakra is the Solar Plexus or *Manipura*.
It is located in the upper abdomen in the stomach area and represents personal power, self-esteem, and confidence. Possible Solar Plexus affirmations include: *I do act with confidence and clarity. I do achieve my financial goals. I do take care of my health and well-being. I do pursue my passions with determination. I do stand in my personal power. I do believe in my ability to succeed. I do make decisions that align with my values.*

SOLAR PLEXUS THIRD

I do

This affirmation empowers my will and determination, aligning my actions with my inner strength.

Threefold Invocation: I arise and declare what I do to the Powers of Me That Be.

1.

2.

3.

Sixfold Affirmation: I pause and repeat what I do to the Powers of Me That Be.

1.

2.

3.

4.

5.

6.

THIRD   SOLAR PLEXUS

I do

This affirmation empowers my will and determination, aligning my actions with my inner strength.

Ninefold Contemplation: I retire and solidify what I do to the Powers of Me That Be.

1.

2.

3.

4.

5.

6.

7.

8.

9.

The third chakra is the Solar Plexus or *Manipura*.

It is located in the upper abdomen in the stomach area and represents personal power, self-esteem, and confidence. Possible Solar Plexus affirmations include: *I do act with confidence and clarity. I do achieve my financial goals. I do take care of my health and well-being. I do pursue my passions with determination. I do stand in my personal power. I do believe in my ability to succeed. I do make decisions that align with my values.*

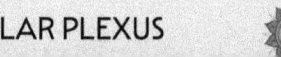

SOLAR PLEXUS   THIRD

I do

This affirmation empowers my will and determination, aligning my actions with my inner strength.

Threefold Invocation: I arise and declare what I do to the Powers of Me That Be.

1.

2.

3.

Sixfold Affirmation: I pause and repeat what I do to the Powers of Me That Be.

1.

2.

3.

4.

5.

6.

I do

This affirmation empowers my will and determination, aligning my actions with my inner strength.

Ninefold Contemplation: I retire and solidify what I do to the Powers of Me That Be.

1.

2.

3.

4.

5.

6.

7.

8.

9.

The third chakra is the Solar Plexus or *Manipura*.
It is located in the upper abdomen in the stomach area and represents personal power, self-esteem, and confidence. Possible Solar Plexus affirmations include: *I do act with confidence and clarity. I do achieve my financial goals. I do take care of my health and well-being. I do pursue my passions with determination. I do stand in my personal power. I do believe in my ability to succeed. I do make decisions that align with my values.*

SOLAR PLEXUS 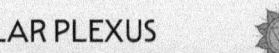 THIRD

I do

This affirmation empowers my will and determination, aligning my actions with my inner strength.

Threefold Invocation: I arise and declare what I do to the Powers of Me That Be.

1.

2.

3.

Sixfold Affirmation: I pause and repeat what I do to the Powers of Me That Be.

1.

2.

3.

4.

5.

6.

THIRD   SOLAR PLEXUS

I do

This affirmation empowers my will and determination, aligning my actions with my inner strength.

Ninefold Contemplation: I retire and solidify what I do to the Powers of Me That Be.

1.

2.

3.

4.

5.

6.

7.

8.

9.

The third chakra is the Solar Plexus or *Manipura*.
It is located in the upper abdomen in the stomach area and represents personal power, self-esteem, and confidence. Possible Solar Plexus affirmations include: *I do act with confidence and clarity. I do achieve my financial goals. I do take care of my health and well-being. I do pursue my passions with determination. I do stand in my personal power. I do believe in my ability to succeed. I do make decisions that align with my values.*

SOLAR PLEXUS  THIRD

I love

This affirmation opens my heart to the universal love, enriching my relationships and inner harmony.

Threefold Invocation: I arise and declare what I love to the Powers of Me That Be.

1.

2.

3.

Sixfold Affirmation: I pause and repeat what I love to the Powers of Me That Be.

1.

2.

3.

4.

5.

6.

FOURTH   HEART

I love

This affirmation opens my heart to the universal love, enriching my relationships and inner harmony.

Ninefold Contemplation: I retire and solidify what I love to the Powers of Me That Be.

1.

2.

3.

4.

5.

6.

7.

8.

9.

The fourth chakra is the Heart or *Anahata*.
It is located in the upper abdomen in the center of the chest near the heart and represents love, compassion, and connection.
Possible Heart affirmations include: *I love myself unconditionally. I love my body and take care of it.
I love and nurture my relationships. I love my career and the opportunities it brings. I love and appreciate
the beauty in the world. I love and accept others as they are. I love the person I am becoming.*

HEART  FOURTH

I love

This affirmation opens my heart to the universal love, enriching my relationships and inner harmony.

Threefold Invocation: I arise and declare what I love to the Powers of Me That Be.

1.

2.

3.

Sixfold Affirmation: I pause and repeat what I love to the Powers of Me That Be.

1.

2.

3.

4.

5.

6.

FOURTH   HEART

I love

This affirmation opens my heart to the universal love, enriching my relationships and inner harmony.

Ninefold Contemplation: I retire and solidify what I love to the Powers of Me That Be.

1.

2.

3.

4.

5.

6.

7.

8.

9.

The fourth chakra is the Heart or *Anahata*.
It is located in the upper abdomen in the center of the chest near the heart and represents love, compassion, and connection.
Possible Heart affirmations include: *I love myself unconditionally. I love my body and take care of it.
I love and nurture my relationships. I love my career and the opportunities it brings. I love and appreciate
the beauty in the world. I love and accept others as they are. I love the person I am becoming.*

HEART  FOURTH

I love

This affirmation opens my heart to the universal love, enriching my relationships and inner harmony.

Threefold Invocation: I arise and declare what I love to the Powers of Me That Be.

1.

2.

3.

Sixfold Affirmation: I pause and repeat what I love to the Powers of Me That Be.

1.

2.

3.

4.

5.

6.

FOURTH　　　HEART

I love

This affirmation opens my heart to the universal love, enriching my relationships and inner harmony.

Ninefold Contemplation: I retire and solidify what I love to the Powers of Me That Be.

1.

2.

3.

4.

5.

6.

7.

8.

9.

The fourth chakra is the Heart or *Anahata*.
It is located in the upper abdomen in the center of the chest near the heart and represents love, compassion, and connection.
Possible Heart affirmations include: *I love myself unconditionally. I love my body and take care of it.
I love and nurture my relationships. I love my career and the opportunities it brings. I love and appreciate
the beauty in the world. I love and accept others as they are. I love the person I am becoming.*

HEART FOURTH

I love

This affirmation opens my heart to the universal love, enriching my relationships and inner harmony.

Threefold Invocation: I arise and declare what I love to the Powers of Me That Be.

1.

2.

3.

Sixfold Affirmation: I pause and repeat what I love to the Powers of Me That Be.

1.

2.

3.

4.

5.

6.

FOURTH   HEART

I love

This affirmation opens my heart to the universal love, enriching my relationships and inner harmony.

Ninefold Contemplation: I retire and solidify what I love to the Powers of Me That Be.

1.

2.

3.

4.

5.

6.

7.

8.

9.

The fourth chakra is the Heart or *Anahata*.
It is located in the upper abdomen in the center of the chest near the heart and represents love, compassion, and connection.
Possible Heart affirmations include: *I love myself unconditionally. I love my body and take care of it.
I love and nurture my relationships. I love my career and the opportunities it brings. I love and appreciate
the beauty in the world. I love and accept others as they are. I love the person I am becoming.*

HEART FOURTH

I love

This affirmation opens my heart to the universal love, enriching my relationships and inner harmony.

Threefold Invocation: I arise and declare what I love to the Powers of Me That Be.

1.

2.

3.

Sixfold Affirmation: I pause and repeat what I love to the Powers of Me That Be.

1.

2.

3.

4.

5.

6.

FOURTH   HEART

I love

This affirmation opens my heart to the universal love, enriching my relationships and inner harmony.

Ninefold Contemplation: I retire and solidify what I love to the Powers of Me That Be.

1.

2.

3.

4.

5.

6.

7.

8.

9.

The fourth chakra is the Heart or *Anahata*.
It is located in the upper abdomen in the center of the chest near the heart and represents love, compassion, and connection.
Possible Heart affirmations include: *I love myself unconditionally. I love my body and take care of it.
I love and nurture my relationships. I love my career and the opportunities it brings. I love and appreciate
the beauty in the world. I love and accept others as they are. I love the person I am becoming.*

HEART FOURTH

I love

This affirmation opens my heart to the universal love, enriching my relationships and inner harmony.

Threefold Invocation: I arise and declare what I love to the Powers of Me That Be.

1.

2.

3.

Sixfold Affirmation: I pause and repeat what I love to the Powers of Me That Be.

1.

2.

3.

4.

5.

6.

FOURTH   HEART

I love

This affirmation opens my heart to the universal love, enriching my relationships and inner harmony.

Ninefold Contemplation: I retire and solidify what I love to the Powers of Me That Be.

1.

2.

3.

4.

5.

6.

7.

8.

9.

The fourth chakra is the Heart or *Anahata*.
It is located in the upper abdomen in the center of the chest near the heart and represents love, compassion, and connection.
Possible Heart affirmations include: *I love myself unconditionally. I love my body and take care of it.
I love and nurture my relationships. I love my career and the opportunities it brings. I love and appreciate
the beauty in the world. I love and accept others as they are. I love the person I am becoming.*

HEART  FOURTH

I love

This affirmation opens my heart to the universal love, enriching my relationships and inner harmony.

Threefold Invocation: I arise and declare what I love to the Powers of Me That Be.

1.

2.

3.

Sixfold Affirmation: I pause and repeat what I love to the Powers of Me That Be.

1.

2.

3.

4.

5.

6.

FOURTH   HEART

I love

This affirmation opens my heart to the universal love, enriching my relationships and inner harmony.

Ninefold Contemplation: I retire and solidify what I love to the Powers of Me That Be.

1.

2.

3.

4.

5.

6.

7.

8.

9.

The fourth chakra is the Heart or *Anahata*.
It is located in the upper abdomen in the center of the chest near the heart and represents love, compassion, and connection.
Possible Heart affirmations include: *I love myself unconditionally. I love my body and take care of it.
I love and nurture my relationships. I love my career and the opportunities it brings. I love and appreciate
the beauty in the world. I love and accept others as they are. I love the person I am becoming.*

HEART   FOURTH

I love

This affirmation opens my heart to the universal love, enriching my relationships and inner harmony.

Threefold Invocation: I arise and declare what I love to the Powers of Me That Be.

1.

2.

3.

Sixfold Affirmation: I pause and repeat what I love to the Powers of Me That Be.

1.

2.

3.

4.

5.

6.

FOURTH   HEART

I love

This affirmation opens my heart to the universal love, enriching my relationships and inner harmony.

Ninefold Contemplation: I retire and solidify what I love to the Powers of Me That Be.

1.

2.

3.

4.

5.

6.

7.

8.

9.

The fourth chakra is the Heart or *Anahata*.
It is located in the upper abdomen in the center of the chest near the heart and represents love, compassion, and connection.
Possible Heart affirmations include: *I love myself unconditionally. I love my body and take care of it.
I love and nurture my relationships. I love my career and the opportunities it brings. I love and appreciate
the beauty in the world. I love and accept others as they are. I love the person I am becoming.*

HEART  FOURTH

I love

This affirmation opens my heart to the universal love, enriching my relationships and inner harmony.

Threefold Invocation: I arise and declare what I love to the Powers of Me That Be.

1.

2.

3.

Sixfold Affirmation: I pause and repeat what I love to the Powers of Me That Be.

1.

2.

3.

4.

5.

6.

FOURTH   HEART

I love

This affirmation opens my heart to the universal love, enriching my relationships and inner harmony.

Ninefold Contemplation: I retire and solidify what I love to the Powers of Me That Be.

1.

2.

3.

4.

5.

6.

7.

8.

9.

The fourth chakra is the Heart or *Anahata*.
It is located in the upper abdomen in the center of the chest near the heart and represents love, compassion, and connection.
Possible Heart affirmations include: *I love myself unconditionally. I love my body and take care of it.
I love and nurture my relationships. I love my career and the opportunities it brings. I love and appreciate
the beauty in the world. I love and accept others as they are. I love the person I am becoming.*

HEART FOURTH

I speak

This affirmation ensures my voice resonates with authenticity and power, facilitating clear communication.

Threefold Invocation: I arise and declare what I speak to the Powers of Me That Be.

1.

2.

3.

Sixfold Affirmation: I pause and repeat what I speak to the Powers of Me That Be.

1.

2.

3.

4.

5.

6.

FIFTH   THROAT

I speak

This affirmation ensures my voice resonates with authenticity and power, facilitating clear communication.

Ninefold Contemplation: I retire and solidify what I speak to the Powers of Me That Be.

1.

2.

3.

4.

5.

6.

7.

8.

9.

The fifth chakra is the Throat or *Vishuddha*.

It is located in the throat and represents communication, self-expression, and truth.
Possible Throat affirmations include: *I speak my truth with clarity and confidence. I speak words of love and kindness. I speak affirmations of abundance and success. I speak up for my health and well-being. I speak with wisdom and compassion. I speak my desires into existence. I speak from a place of inner truth.*

THROAT FIFTH

I speak

This affirmation ensures my voice resonates with authenticity and power, facilitating clear communication.

Threefold Invocation: I arise and declare what I speak to the Powers of Me That Be.

1.

2.

3.

Sixfold Affirmation: I pause and repeat what I speak to the Powers of Me That Be.

1.

2.

3.

4.

5.

6.

I speak

This affirmation ensures my voice resonates with authenticity and power, facilitating clear communication.

Ninefold Contemplation: I retire and solidify what I speak to the Powers of Me That Be.

1.

2.

3.

4.

5.

6.

7.

8.

9.

The fifth chakra is the Throat or *Vishuddha*.
It is located in the throat and represents communication, self-expression, and truth.
Possible Throat affirmations include: *I speak my truth with clarity and confidence. I speak words of love and kindness. I speak affirmations of abundance and success. I speak up for my health and well-being. I speak with wisdom and compassion. I speak my desires into existence. I speak from a place of inner truth.*

THROAT FIFTH

I speak

This affirmation ensures my voice resonates with authenticity and power, facilitating clear communication.

Threefold Invocation: I arise and declare what I speak to the Powers of Me That Be.

1.

2.

3.

Sixfold Affirmation: I pause and repeat what I speak to the Powers of Me That Be.

1.

2.

3.

4.

5.

6.

FIFTH   THROAT

I speak

This affirmation ensures my voice resonates with authenticity and power, facilitating clear communication.

Ninefold Contemplation: I retire and solidify what I speak to the Powers of Me That Be.

1.

2.

3.

4.

5.

6.

7.

8.

9.

The fifth chakra is the Throat or *Vishuddha*.

It is located in the throat and represents communication, self-expression, and truth.
Possible Throat affirmations include: *I speak my truth with clarity and confidence. I speak words of love and kindness. I speak affirmations of abundance and success. I speak up for my health and well-being. I speak with wisdom and compassion. I speak my desires into existence. I speak from a place of inner truth.*

THROAT   FIFTH

I speak

This affirmation ensures my voice resonates with authenticity and power, facilitating clear communication.

Threefold Invocation: I arise and declare what I speak to the Powers of Me That Be.

1.

2.

3.

Sixfold Affirmation: I pause and repeat what I speak to the Powers of Me That Be.

1.

2.

3.

4.

5.

6.

FIFTH   THROAT

I speak

This affirmation ensures my voice resonates with authenticity and power, facilitating clear communication.

Ninefold Contemplation: I retire and solidify what I speak to the Powers of Me That Be.

1.

2.

3.

4.

5.

6.

7.

8.

9.

The fifth chakra is the Throat or *Vishuddha*.

It is located in the throat and represents communication, self-expression, and truth.
Possible Throat affirmations include: *I speak my truth with clarity and confidence. I speak words of love and kindness. I speak affirmations of abundance and success. I speak up for my health and well-being. I speak with wisdom and compassion. I speak my desires into existence. I speak from a place of inner truth.*

THROAT FIFTH

I speak

This affirmation ensures my voice resonates with authenticity and power, facilitating clear communication.

Threefold Invocation: I arise and declare what I speak to the Powers of Me That Be.

1.

2.

3.

Sixfold Affirmation: I pause and repeat what I speak to the Powers of Me That Be.

1.

2.

3.

4.

5.

6.

FIFTH   THROAT

I speak

This affirmation ensures my voice resonates with authenticity and power, facilitating clear communication.

Ninefold Contemplation: I retire and solidify what I speak to the Powers of Me That Be.

1.

2.

3.

4.

5.

6.

7.

8.

9.

The fifth chakra is the Throat or *Vishuddha*.

It is located in the throat and represents communication, self-expression, and truth.
Possible Throat affirmations include: *I speak my truth with clarity and confidence. I speak words of love and kindness. I speak affirmations of abundance and success. I speak up for my health and well-being. I speak with wisdom and compassion. I speak my desires into existence. I speak from a place of inner truth.*

THROAT   FIFTH

I speak

This affirmation ensures my voice resonates with authenticity and power, facilitating clear communication.

Threefold Invocation: I arise and declare what I speak to the Powers of Me That Be.

1.

2.

3.

Sixfold Affirmation: I pause and repeat what I speak to the Powers of Me That Be.

1.

2.

3.

4.

5.

6.

FIFTH   THROAT

I speak

This affirmation ensures my voice resonates with authenticity and power, facilitating clear communication.

Ninefold Contemplation: I retire and solidify what I speak to the Powers of Me That Be.

1.

2.

3.

4.

5.

6.

7.

8.

9.

The fifth chakra is the Throat or *Vishuddha*.
It is located in the throat and represents communication, self-expression, and truth.
Possible Throat affirmations include: *I speak my truth with clarity and confidence. I speak words of love and kindness. I speak affirmations of abundance and success. I speak up for my health and well-being. I speak with wisdom and compassion. I speak my desires into existence. I speak from a place of inner truth.*

THROAT FIFTH

I speak

This affirmation ensures my voice resonates with authenticity and power, facilitating clear communication.

Threefold Invocation: I arise and declare what I speak to the Powers of Me That Be.

1.

2.

3.

Sixfold Affirmation: I pause and repeat what I speak to the Powers of Me That Be.

1.

2.

3.

4.

5.

6.

FIFTH   THROAT

I speak

This affirmation ensures my voice resonates with authenticity and power, facilitating clear communication.

Ninefold Contemplation: I retire and solidify what I speak to the Powers of Me That Be.

1.

2.

3.

4.

5.

6.

7.

8.

9.

The fifth chakra is the Throat or *Vishuddha*.
It is located in the throat and represents communication, self-expression, and truth.
Possible Throat affirmations include: *I speak my truth with clarity and confidence. I speak words of love and kindness. I speak affirmations of abundance and success. I speak up for my health and well-being. I speak with wisdom and compassion. I speak my desires into existence. I speak from a place of inner truth.*

THROAT FIFTH

I speak

This affirmation ensures my voice resonates with authenticity and power, facilitating clear communication.

Threefold Invocation: I arise and declare what I speak to the Powers of Me That Be.

1.

2.

3.

Sixfold Affirmation: I pause and repeat what I speak to the Powers of Me That Be.

1.

2.

3.

4.

5.

6.

FIFTH   THROAT

I speak

This affirmation ensures my voice resonates with authenticity and power, facilitating clear communication.

Ninefold Contemplation: I retire and solidify what I speak to the Powers of Me That Be.

1.

2.

3.

4.

5.

6.

7.

8.

9.

The fifth chakra is the Throat or *Vishuddha*.

It is located in the throat and represents communication, self-expression, and truth. Possible Throat affirmations include: *I speak my truth with clarity and confidence. I speak words of love and kindness. I speak affirmations of abundance and success. I speak up for my health and well-being. I speak with wisdom and compassion. I speak my desires into existence. I speak from a place of inner truth.*

THROAT FIFTH

I speak

This affirmation ensures my voice resonates with authenticity and power, facilitating clear communication.

Threefold Invocation: I arise and declare what I speak to the Powers of Me That Be.

1.

2.

3.

Sixfold Affirmation: I pause and repeat what I speak to the Powers of Me That Be.

1.

2.

3.

4.

5.

6.

FIFTH   THROAT

I speak

This affirmation ensures my voice resonates with authenticity and power, facilitating clear communication.

Ninefold Contemplation: I retire and solidify what I speak to the Powers of Me That Be.

1.

2.

3.

4.

5.

6.

7.

8.

9.

The fifth chakra is the Throat or *Vishuddha*.

It is located in the throat and represents communication, self-expression, and truth.
Possible Throat affirmations include: *I speak my truth with clarity and confidence. I speak words of love and kindness. I speak affirmations of abundance and success. I speak up for my health and well-being. I speak with wisdom and compassion. I speak my desires into existence. I speak from a place of inner truth.*

THROAT FIFTH

I see

This affirmation enhances my perception and wisdom, allowing me to navigate life with greater clarity.

Threefold Invocation: I arise and declare what I see to the Powers of Me That Be.

1.

2.

3.

Sixfold Affirmation: I pause and repeat what I see to The Powers of Me that be.

1.

2.

3.

4.

5.

6.

SIXTH   THIRD EYE

I see

This affirmation enhances my perception and wisdom, allowing me to navigate life with greater clarity.

Ninefold Contemplation: I retire and solidify what I see to the Powers of Me That Be.

1.

2.

3.

4.

5.

6.

7.

8.

9.

The sixth chakra is the Third Eye or *Ajna*.

It is located in the forehead between the eyes and represents intuition, insight, and wisdom. Possible Third Eye affirmations include: *I see the path to my financial success clearly. I see the beauty and goodness in others. I see solutions to my health challenges. I see opportunities for growth and learning. I see my dreams becoming reality. I see my life with clarity and purpose. I see abundance and prosperity flowing to me.*

THIRD EYE SIXTH

I see

This affirmation enhances my perception and wisdom, allowing me to navigate life with greater clarity.

Threefold Invocation: I arise and declare what I see to the Powers of Me That Be.

1.

2.

3.

Sixfold Affirmation: I pause and repeat what I see to The Powers of Me that be.

1.

2.

3.

4.

5.

6.

SIXTH THIRD EYE

I see

This affirmation enhances my perception and wisdom, allowing me to navigate life with greater clarity.

Ninefold Contemplation: I retire and solidify what I see to the Powers of Me That Be.

1.

2.

3.

4.

5.

6.

7.

8.

9.

The sixth chakra is the Third Eye or *Ajna*.

It is located in the forehead between the eyes and represents intuition, insight, and wisdom. Possible Third Eye affirmations include: *I see the path to my financial success clearly. I see the beauty and goodness in others. I see solutions to my health challenges. I see opportunities for growth and learning. I see my dreams becoming reality. I see my life with clarity and purpose. I see abundance and prosperity flowing to me.*

THIRD EYE SIXTH

I see

This affirmation enhances my perception and wisdom, allowing me to navigate life with greater clarity.

Threefold Invocation: I arise and declare what I see to the Powers of Me That Be.

1.

2.

3.

Sixfold Affirmation: I pause and repeat what I see to The Powers of Me that be.

1.

2.

3.

4.

5.

6.

SIXTH   THIRD EYE

I see

This affirmation enhances my perception and wisdom, allowing me to navigate life with greater clarity.

Ninefold Contemplation: I retire and solidify what I see to the Powers of Me That Be.

1.

2.

3.

4.

5.

6.

7.

8.

9.

The sixth chakra is the Third Eye or *Ajna*.

It is located in the forehead between the eyes and represents intuition, insight, and wisdom. Possible Third Eye affirmations include: *I see the path to my financial success clearly. I see the beauty and goodness in others. I see solutions to my health challenges. I see opportunities for growth and learning. I see my dreams becoming reality. I see my life with clarity and purpose. I see abundance and prosperity flowing to me.*

THIRD EYE SIXTH

I see

This affirmation enhances my perception and wisdom, allowing me to navigate life with greater clarity.

Threefold Invocation: I arise and declare what I see to the Powers of Me That Be.

1.

2.

3.

Sixfold Affirmation: I pause and repeat what I see to The Powers of Me that be.

1.

2.

3.

4.

5.

6.

SIXTH THIRD EYE

I see

This affirmation enhances my perception and wisdom, allowing me to navigate life with greater clarity.

Ninefold Contemplation: I retire and solidify what I see to the Powers of Me That Be.

1.

2.

3.

4.

5.

6.

7.

8.

9.

The sixth chakra is the Third Eye or *Ajna*.

It is located in the forehead between the eyes and represents intuition, insight, and wisdom. Possible Third Eye affirmations include: *I see the path to my financial success clearly. I see the beauty and goodness in others. I see solutions to my health challenges. I see opportunities for growth and learning. I see my dreams becoming reality. I see my life with clarity and purpose. I see abundance and prosperity flowing to me.*

THIRD EYE SIXTH

I see

This affirmation enhances my perception and wisdom, allowing me to navigate life with greater clarity.

Threefold Invocation: I arise and declare what I see to the Powers of Me That Be.

1.

2.

3.

Sixfold Affirmation: I pause and repeat what I see to The Powers of Me that be.

1.

2.

3.

4.

5.

6.

SIXTH   THIRD EYE

I see

This affirmation enhances my perception and wisdom, allowing me to navigate life with greater clarity.

Ninefold Contemplation: I retire and solidify what I see to the Powers of Me That Be.

1.

2.

3.

4.

5.

6.

7.

8.

9.

The sixth chakra is the Third Eye or *Ajna*.

It is located in the forehead between the eyes and represents intuition, insight, and wisdom. Possible Third Eye affirmations include: *I see the path to my financial success clearly. I see the beauty and goodness in others. I see solutions to my health challenges. I see opportunities for growth and learning. I see my dreams becoming reality. I see my life with clarity and purpose. I see abundance and prosperity flowing to me.*

 SIXTH

I see

This affirmation enhances my perception and wisdom, allowing me to navigate life with greater clarity.

Threefold Invocation: I arise and declare what I see to the Powers of Me That Be.

1.

2.

3.

Sixfold Affirmation: I pause and repeat what I see to The Powers of Me that be.

1.

2.

3.

4.

5.

6.

SIXTH  THIRD EYE

I see

This affirmation enhances my perception and wisdom, allowing me to navigate life with greater clarity.

Ninefold Contemplation: I retire and solidify what I see to the Powers of Me That Be.

1.

2.

3.

4.

5.

6.

7.

8.

9.

The sixth chakra is the Third Eye or *Ajna*.

It is located in the forehead between the eyes and represents intuition, insight, and wisdom. Possible Third Eye affirmations include: *I see the path to my financial success clearly. I see the beauty and goodness in others. I see solutions to my health challenges. I see opportunities for growth and learning. I see my dreams becoming reality. I see my life with clarity and purpose. I see abundance and prosperity flowing to me.*

THIRD EYE SIXTH

I see

This affirmation enhances my perception and wisdom, allowing me to navigate life with greater clarity.

Threefold Invocation: I arise and declare what I see to the Powers of Me That Be.

1.

2.

3.

Sixfold Affirmation: I pause and repeat what I see to The Powers of Me that be.

1.

2.

3.

4.

5.

6.

SIXTH   THIRD EYE

I see

This affirmation enhances my perception and wisdom, allowing me to navigate life with greater clarity.

Ninefold Contemplation: I retire and solidify what I see to the Powers of Me That Be.

1.

2.

3.

4.

5.

6.

7.

8.

9.

The sixth chakra is the Third Eye or *Ajna*.

It is located in the forehead between the eyes and represents intuition, insight, and wisdom. Possible Third Eye affirmations include: *I see the path to my financial success clearly. I see the beauty and goodness in others. I see solutions to my health challenges. I see opportunities for growth and learning. I see my dreams becoming reality. I see my life with clarity and purpose. I see abundance and prosperity flowing to me.*

THIRD EYE SIXTH

I see

This affirmation enhances my perception and wisdom, allowing me to navigate life with greater clarity.

Threefold Invocation: I arise and declare what I see to the Powers of Me That Be.

1.

2.

3.

Sixfold Affirmation: I pause and repeat what I see to The Powers of Me that be.

1.

2.

3.

4.

5.

6.

SIXTH THIRD EYE

I see

This affirmation enhances my perception and wisdom, allowing me to navigate life with greater clarity.

Ninefold Contemplation: I retire and solidify what I see to the Powers of Me That Be.

1.

2.

3.

4.

5.

6.

7.

8.

9.

The sixth chakra is the Third Eye or *Ajna.*

It is located in the forehead between the eyes and represents intuition, insight, and wisdom.
Possible Third Eye affirmations include: *I see the path to my financial success clearly. I see the beauty and goodness in others. I see solutions to my health challenges. I see opportunities for growth and learning. I see my dreams becoming reality. I see my life with clarity and purpose. I see abundance and prosperity flowing to me.*

THIRD EYE   SIXTH

I see

This affirmation enhances my perception and wisdom, allowing me to navigate life with greater clarity.

Threefold Invocation: I arise and declare what I see to the Powers of Me That Be.

1.

2.

3.

Sixfold Affirmation: I pause and repeat what I see to The Powers of Me that be.

1.

2.

3.

4.

5.

6.

SIXTH   THIRD EYE

I see

This affirmation enhances my perception and wisdom, allowing me to navigate life with greater clarity.

Ninefold Contemplation: I retire and solidify what I see to the Powers of Me That Be.

1.

2.

3.

4.

5.

6.

7.

8.

9.

The sixth chakra is the Third Eye or *Ajna*.

It is located in the forehead between the eyes and represents intuition, insight, and wisdom.
Possible Third Eye affirmations include: *I see the path to my financial success clearly. I see the beauty and goodness in others. I see solutions to my health challenges. I see opportunities for growth and learning. I see my dreams becoming reality. I see my life with clarity and purpose. I see abundance and prosperity flowing to me.*

THIRD EYE   SIXTH

I understand

This affirmation connects me to the higher consciousness, fostering spiritual enlightenment and unity.

Threefold Invocation: I arise and declare what I understand to the Powers of Me That Be.

1.

2.

3.

Sixfold Affirmation: I pause and repeat what I understand to the Powers of Me That Be.

1.

2.

3.

4.

5.

6.

SEVENTH   CROWN

I understand

This affirmation connects me to the higher consciousness, fostering spiritual enlightenment and unity.

Ninefold Contemplation: I retire and solidify what I understand to the Powers of Me That Be.

1.

2.

3.

4.

5.

6.

7.

8.

9.

The seventh chakra is the Crown or *Sahasrara*.

It is located on the top of the head and represents spiritual connection, enlightenment, and higher consciousness.
Possible Crown affirmations include: *I understand that I am connected to the universe. I understand the importance of health and balance. I understand the flow of financial abundance. I understand the value of loving relationships. I understand my purpose and mission in life. I understand the wisdom of my experiences. I understand the power of my thoughts.*

CROWN   SEVENTH

I understand

This affirmation connects me to the higher consciousness, fostering spiritual enlightenment and unity.

Threefold Invocation: I arise and declare what I understand to the Powers of Me That Be.

1.

2.

3.

Sixfold Affirmation: I pause and repeat what I understand to the Powers of Me That Be.

1.

2.

3.

4.

5.

6.

SEVENTH   CROWN

I understand

This affirmation connects me to the higher consciousness, fostering spiritual enlightenment and unity.

Ninefold Contemplation: I retire and solidify what I understand to the Powers of Me That Be.

1.

2.

3.

4.

5.

6.

7.

8.

9.

The seventh chakra is the Crown or *Sahasrara*.

It is located on the top of the head and represents spiritual connection, enlightenment, and higher consciousness.
Possible Crown affirmations include: *I understand that I am connected to the universe. I understand the importance
of health and balance. I understand the flow of financial abundance. I understand the value of loving relationships.
I understand my purpose and mission in life. I understand the wisdom of my experiences.
I understand the power of my thoughts.*

CROWN   SEVENTH

I understand

This affirmation connects me to the higher consciousness, fostering spiritual enlightenment and unity.

Threefold Invocation: I arise and declare what I understand to the Powers of Me That Be.

1.

2.

3.

Sixfold Affirmation: I pause and repeat what I understand to the Powers of Me That Be.

1.

2.

3.

4.

5.

6.

SEVENTH   CROWN

I understand

This affirmation connects me to the higher consciousness, fostering spiritual enlightenment and unity.

Ninefold Contemplation: I retire and solidify what I understand to the Powers of Me That Be.

1.

2.

3.

4.

5.

6.

7.

8.

9.

The seventh chakra is the Crown or *Sahasrara.*

It is located on the top of the head and represents spiritual connection, enlightenment, and higher consciousness.
Possible Crown affirmations include: *I understand that I am connected to the universe. I understand the importance of health and balance. I understand the flow of financial abundance. I understand the value of loving relationships. I understand my purpose and mission in life. I understand the wisdom of my experiences. I understand the power of my thoughts.*

CROWN   SEVENTH

I understand

This affirmation connects me to the higher consciousness, fostering spiritual enlightenment and unity.

Threefold Invocation: I arise and declare what I understand to the Powers of Me That Be.

1.

2.

3.

Sixfold Affirmation: I pause and repeat what I understand to the Powers of Me That Be.

1.

2.

3.

4.

5.

6.

SEVENTH   CROWN

I understand

This affirmation connects me to the higher consciousness, fostering spiritual enlightenment and unity.

Ninefold Contemplation: I retire and solidify what I understand to the Powers of Me That Be.

1.

2.

3.

4.

5.

6.

7.

8.

9.

The seventh chakra is the Crown or *Sahasrara.*

It is located on the top of the head and represents spiritual connection, enlightenment, and higher consciousness.
Possible Crown affirmations include: *I understand that I am connected to the universe. I understand the importance of health and balance. I understand the flow of financial abundance. I understand the value of loving relationships. I understand my purpose and mission in life. I understand the wisdom of my experiences. I understand the power of my thoughts.*

CROWN   SEVENTH

I understand

This affirmation connects me to the higher consciousness, fostering spiritual enlightenment and unity.

Threefold Invocation: I arise and declare what I understand to the Powers of Me That Be.

1.

2.

3.

Sixfold Affirmation: I pause and repeat what I understand to the Powers of Me That Be.

1.

2.

3.

4.

5.

6.

SEVENTH   CROWN

I understand

This affirmation connects me to the higher consciousness, fostering spiritual enlightenment and unity.

Ninefold Contemplation: I retire and solidify what I understand to the Powers of Me That Be.

1.

2.

3.

4.

5.

6.

7.

8.

9.

The seventh chakra is the Crown or *Sahasrara.*

It is located on the top of the head and represents spiritual connection, enlightenment, and higher consciousness.
Possible Crown affirmations include: *I understand that I am connected to the universe. I understand the importance of health and balance. I understand the flow of financial abundance. I understand the value of loving relationships. I understand my purpose and mission in life. I understand the wisdom of my experiences. I understand the power of my thoughts.*

CROWN   SEVENTH

I understand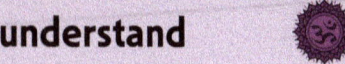

This affirmation connects me to the higher consciousness, fostering spiritual enlightenment and unity.

Threefold Invocation: I arise and declare what I understand to the Powers of Me That Be.

1.

2.

3.

Sixfold Affirmation: I pause and repeat what I understand to the Powers of Me That Be.

1.

2.

3.

4.

5.

6.

SEVENTH   CROWN

I understand

This affirmation connects me to the higher consciousness, fostering spiritual enlightenment and unity.

Ninefold Contemplation: I retire and solidify what I understand to the Powers of Me That Be.

1.

2.

3.

4.

5.

6.

7.

8.

9.

The seventh chakra is the Crown or *Sahasrara.*

It is located on the top of the head and represents spiritual connection, enlightenment, and higher consciousness.
Possible Crown affirmations include: *I understand that I am connected to the universe. I understand the importance of health and balance. I understand the flow of financial abundance. I understand the value of loving relationships. I understand my purpose and mission in life. I understand the wisdom of my experiences. I understand the power of my thoughts.*

CROWN   SEVENTH

I understand

This affirmation connects me to the higher consciousness, fostering spiritual enlightenment and unity

Threefold Invocation: I arise and declare what I understand to the Powers of Me That Be.

1.

2.

3.

Sixfold Affirmation: I pause and repeat what I understand to the Powers of Me That Be.

1.

2.

3.

4.

5.

6.

SEVENTH   CROWN

I understand

This affirmation connects me to the higher consciousness, fostering spiritual enlightenment and unity.

Ninefold Contemplation: I retire and solidify what I understand to the Powers of Me That Be.

1.

2.

3.

4.

5.

6.

7.

8.

9.

The seventh chakra is the Crown or *Sahasrara.*

It is located on the top of the head and represents spiritual connection, enlightenment, and higher consciousness.
Possible Crown affirmations include: *I understand that I am connected to the universe. I understand the importance of health and balance. I understand the flow of financial abundance. I understand the value of loving relationships. I understand my purpose and mission in life. I understand the wisdom of my experiences. I understand the power of my thoughts.*

CROWN   SEVENTH

I understand

This affirmation connects me to the higher consciousness, fostering spiritual enlightenment and unity.

Threefold Invocation: I arise and declare what I understand to the Powers of Me That Be.

1.

2.

3.

Sixfold Affirmation: I pause and repeat what I understand to the Powers of Me That Be.

1.

2.

3.

4.

5.

6.

SEVENTH   CROWN

I understand

This affirmation connects me to the higher consciousness, fostering spiritual enlightenment and unity.

Ninefold Contemplation: I retire and solidify what I understand to the Powers of Me That Be.

1.

2.

3.

4.

5.

6.

7.

8.

9.

The seventh chakra is the Crown or *Sahasrara*.

It is located on the top of the head and represents spiritual connection, enlightenment, and higher consciousness.
Possible Crown affirmations include: *I understand that I am connected to the universe. I understand the importance of health and balance. I understand the flow of financial abundance. I understand the value of loving relationships. I understand my purpose and mission in life. I understand the wisdom of my experiences. I understand the power of my thoughts.*

CROWN   SEVENTH

I understand

This affirmation connects me to the higher consciousness, fostering spiritual enlightenment and unity.

Threefold Invocation: I arise and declare what I understand to the Powers of Me That Be.

1.

2.

3.

Sixfold Affirmation: I pause and repeat what I understand to the Powers of Me That Be.

1.

2.

3.

4.

5.

6.

SEVENTH   CROWN

I understand

This affirmation connects me to the higher consciousness, fostering spiritual enlightenment and unity.

Ninefold Contemplation: I retire and solidify what I understand to the Powers of Me That Be.

1.

2.

3.

4.

5.

6.

7.

8.

9.

The seventh chakra is the Crown or *Sahasrara*.

It is located on the top of the head and represents spiritual connection, enlightenment, and higher consciousness.
Possible Crown affirmations include: *I understand that I am connected to the universe. I understand the importance of health and balance. I understand the flow of financial abundance. I understand the value of loving relationships. I understand my purpose and mission in life. I understand the wisdom of my experiences. I understand the power of my thoughts.*

CROWN   SEVENTH

"The Powers of Me That Be: 3-6-9 Chakra Affirmation Workbook" copyright 2024 by Emilio Hallivan

All rights reserved. No part of this book may be reproduced in any form whatsoever, by photography or xerography or by any other means, by broadcast or transmission, by translation into any kind of language, nor by recording electronically or otherwise, without permission in writing from the author, except by a reviewer, who may quote brief passages in critical articles or reviews.

ISBN 13: 978-1-64343-523-7

Library of Congress Catalog Number: TK

Printed in the United States of America
First Printing: 2024

28 27 26 25 24   5 4 3 2 1

Cover and interior design by Aleah Salloway

Beaver's Pond Press, Inc.
939 Seventh Street West
Saint Paul, Minnesota 55102
(952) 829-8818
www.BeaversPondPress.com

www.ingramcontent.com/pod-product-compliance
Lightning Source LLC
Chambersburg PA
CBHW040639100526